WRITING REVERSE HAREM FOR FUN & MONEY

A Rage Against the Manuscript guide

STEFF GREEN

ISBN: 978-0-9951222-0-8

Created with Vellum

ARE YOU READY TO WRITE YOUR REVERSE HAREM NOVEL?

Reverse harem books are hot in the charts right now. Although stories about falling in love with more than one person have always been around, the trope of one woman having multiple male partners has been having a moment in the spotlight recently.

Since 2016, reverse harem has become a common term used by readers to identify a type of book where a heroine acquires a 'harem' of +3 guys who are all utterly devoted to her. Unlike a love triangle where the heroine has to choose one lover in the end, in a reverse harem, she gets her "happily ever after" with all of them.

2017 was the year reverse harem novels really started to tear up the charts. Several best-selling series made it into the Amazon top 100 and reverse harem titles have become available in all genres of romance – and even several non-romance. Fueled by an active social media presence and an army of voracious readers, reverse harem books are still going strong. In fact, they're more popular than ever.

Readers love these stories because of the wish-fulfilment

factor. How amazing would it be to have not one devoted guy at your beck and call, but five? Having more than one hero also enables authors to explore personality types beyond the typical alpha male, leading to more diversity and interest.

This upstart new genre is on the verge of becoming evergreen, and the fans are still demanding more. Reverse harem isn't going away any time soon.

For a writer, reverse harem can be an exciting challenge. I love being able to write different types of heroes. I'm a sucker for tortured artist-types, and in reverse harem, these characters get their chance to shine alongside more typical alpha males.

I also love the diversity of stories and settings and worlds, and the challenge of creating a situation that would foster this unusual type of relationship.

Oh, and the sex is fun to write, too.

If you're excited to write your own reverse harem, I've created this resource to pull together some tips and tricks I've learned since I started publishing these books. As a six-figure author of two popular reverse harem series (under my pen name, Steffanie Holmes), I'll show you how to craft a story your readers will love, and how to make sure those readers can find your books. I'll give you the best tools to help you reach success, and have fun at the same time.

Are you ready? Let's get writing!

ABOUT ME

Just so you know I'm not talking out my arse, I'll tell you a little about my writing career and success with reverse harem.

I'm Steff, and I've been self-publishing my work since 2014. I started off writing super series science fiction novels in the vein of China Mieville. These sold at the rate of 2-3 copies per month.

One day, I attended a party where a friend and I were discussing *50 Shades of Grey*. This friend loved the books, and I'd read the first chapter and couldn't continue because of the writing style and grammar (or lack thereof).

I was having a bitch about this book's success, when my friend cut in to say, "It's not as if you could write a sexy book like that, Steff."

I nodded in agreement and changed the subject, because of course she was right. In my group of very sexually adventurous friends, I'm known for being quite private about my sex life and, well, I can't say the word 'penis' without blushing. But in my head, the cogs were turning.

Challenge accepted.

In secret, without telling anyone, I wrote a 30,000-word story about a fox shapeshifter named Ryan who lived as a reclusive artist, and the gallery curator who brought him out of his shell. There's a shifter war and an unhinged brother and a crumbling medieval manor and all sorts of intrigue. I paid $50 for a cover and published it in April 2015 under a secret pen name – Steffanie Holmes. I expected nothing to happen except that one day when I wasn't mortified about the sex in it I could show it to my friend and we'd both have a laugh.

I sold 1000 copies in the first week.

I couldn't believe it. I kept expecting Amazon to call me to say they'd given me someone else's royalties by mistake. But they never called and the sales kept coming. I had to sheepishly tell my husband that I'd made all this money from my books, but it wasn't from the science fiction, it was from this smutty fox shifter romance story.

After he got done laughing, he said, "So, are you going to write more?"

Fast-forward to now. I've published 30 books in total, most of them paranormal romance novels as Steffanie Holmes. I quit my day job in Feb 2018 in order to live the dream life of a full-time writer. I earn six-figures a year from my writing and have the most incredible fun doing it. I am so insanely lucky and grateful and that's why I've written this guide – because I want you to be able to share in the joy of telling stories of the heart and seeing your writing find an audience.

MY REVERSE HAREM BOOKS

A week after I left my day job, I released my first reverse harem novel, *The Castle of Earth and Embers,* book 1 of the Briarwood Witches series. Up until this point, I'd been doing well off the back of my previous paranormal romance novels, but it's thanks to this series that my career took off.

Before the book's release, I was earning between $1000-3000 per month on Amazon, and about $1000 on the other stores. Since I started releasing the Briarwood Witches books, my income climbed to $4k, $6k, $10k, and up.

I released 5 books in that series throughout 2018, approximately 1 book every 2 months. In December 2018, I released the box set of the complete series.

In January of 2019, I released book one in my new Nevermore Bookshop Mysteries series, *A Dead and Stormy Night.* What's been interesting about this series is that it doesn't follow the typical conventions of a romance book. I planned it based around a cozy mystery plot, but with reverse harem elements. It was a gamble, but that gamble paid off – the Nevermore Bookshop series has been even more successful so far than the Briarwood Witches, and it's so much fun to write.

Throughout this book, I'll be referring to both my series, as these are readily available sources for examples. You might like to read them to see how I put the lessons in this book into practice in order to create a six-figure income from reverse harem. I'll also refer to other reverse harem books, which you'll find in the suggested reading list at the back of this guide.

Chapter One

WHAT IS A REVERSE HAREM ROMANCE?

I discovered reverse harem as a reader at the end of 2017. I'd been hearing the phrase pop up in writing conversations for a few months, but I wasn't that interested until a writer friend raved about the Rock Hard Beautiful series by CM Stunich. A rockstar romance where the girl ends up with the whole band? That's my kind of story!

I devoured the three books in that series in a weekend and went hunting for more. What I discovered was not a one-off wonder but a whole world of unique settings, strong female characters, and harems of guys who worship them.

I joined groups on Facebook dedicated to discussing all things reverse harem and discovered that the trope actually started in anime, manga, and otome games. In reverse harem anime, the girl has a group of guys who exist around her (and may or may not be in love with her). In the end, she has to choose one of them. Some of the best reverse harem anime are *Uta no Prince-sama!*, *Fruits Basket*, and *Ouran High School Host Club*.

Some women watching or reading reverse harem anime and manga got sick of the idea of the girl having to choose between all the guys. Too often you'd end up hating the guy she actually did choose or wishing it was a different kind of story all-together. Guys in stories got to have harems of women who all share, so why couldn't it work in reverse?

Some of those fans started writing their own stories where the female main character didn't have to choose. These fans might also have been reading *Twilight* or *The Hunger Games* (wishing Bella and Katniss didn't have to choose) or books by Laurell K Hamilton (whose popular vampire series is one of the earliest reverse harem stories).

Early writers like CL Stone and BL Brunnemer self-published their work (which definitely has an anime influence in the stories and mannerisms of the characters). The readers demanded more more more. This started reverse harem as a book genre (with the key difference being that the heroine has her happily-ever-after with *all* the heroes), as well as the associated hashtag #whychoose.

Reverse harem readers are greedy – they want it all. All the guys, all the feels, all the sex, all the heartbreaks, and heartthrobs. They love reverse harem in all its different facets – some of the books are aimed at a young adult audience, with teenage protagonists who might not even kiss until book six (CL Stone, B L Brunnemer). Others are hyper-steamy with the sexual tension and bedroom acrobatics turned up to 11 (CM Stunich, Tate James, Steffanie Holmes).

Many reverse harem books feature some element of the paranormal, but there are lots of hot contemporary titles as well (one of my favorites being Bethany Jadin's series, The Code). Reverse harem books also appear in other romance genres – historical, fantasy, science fiction – and even non-romance genres like urban fantasy, high fantasy, and cozy mystery.

Reverse harem books are becoming more and more popular. I love this in part because it helps to normalize polyamory and different types of relationships. Many reverse harem books involve elements of bisexuality and homosexuality, and often tackle difficult issues as characters struggle to come to terms with being who they are. I love the diversity in the books and how they showcase something many of us might consider kinky or creepy as truly beautiful and life-affirming.

Let's dive into the unique elements that define reverse harem.

ELEMENTS OF A REVERSE HAREM NOVEL

Point of view: Most reverse harem books are written in first person, with alternating POV chapters. Most of the chapters are from the heroine's POV, with some from the guys. A few reverse harem books are in third (Alex Liddell's *Power of Five*, for example – although this combines 1st and 3rd POV), and some are only from the heroine's POV (The Nevermore Bookshop series).

Tense: Past and present tense are both common.

Series: Most reverse harem novels follow a typical fantasy series arc with the same characters battling a big bad with cliffhangers between volumes, instead of a romance series format where a new couple is introduced in every book. (more on this later).

Female heroine: A reverse harem novel wouldn't be complete without a heroine to be the center of the world. She's the protagonist, and she's the one who drives the story. She's also the one around which all the guys (who may not always get on) rally.

Reverse harem protagonists have a lot of inner strength. You have to be strong in order to handle this many male egos! The heroine has an equal amount of love for all of the men because each of them fills a particular emotional need. For example, in my Briarwood Witches series, Maeve needs

Corbin in order to bounce ideas off and puzzle out the mysteries of Briarwood Castle, while Arthur helps her to realize her inner strength.

Your heroine probably has a dark past that leads to relationship issues – an abusive household, sexual assault, grief, etc. She's hurting, but she might not realize it yet. Her men are going to help her to heal herself, and her love will heal them.

She might be hesitant to love, especially to love more than one guy. She doesn't know what to do or how to choose. This will likely be an initial source of conflict in your book.

3 or more heroes (aka, the harem): You want three or more love interests for your heroine to collect. The number you choose is up to you. Most reverse harem books include 3-5 heroes, but some have many more. (CM Stunich's Harem of Hearts series includes nine!) Remember that the more you have, the harder it might be to give each of them a satisfying emotional arc. Also, if you're writing explicit sex scenes, then more than four guys might leave several heroes without anything to do!

Make your guys as distinct in looks and personality as possible. Here, you're able to step outside the typical romance alpha male heroes and explore other personality types, so take advantage of that. Think about beta guys, tortured souls, protectors, outlaws, nerds, jokers, poets, guys who aren't conventionally attractive, guys with physical or mental disabilities, etc. Many authors like to look at Jungian archetypes or Myers-Briggs personality types to compose their heroes.

Usually, the guys already have some kind of relationship in the beginning of the book. In Nevermore Bookshop, Heathcliff, Morrie, and Quoth have been living together as friends before they meet Mina. In BL Brunnemer's Veil Diaries series, the guys are all high school friends who 'adopt' the heroine Lexie. In KT Strange's Rogue Witch series, the guys are all werewolves and all members of the band Phoenixcry. However, that doesn't mean you can't throw in a surprise or two. In Briarwood Witches, four of the guys are close friends, and I throw in a random stranger, Blake, at the end of book 1 to shake things up. Not all of the guys accept Blake right away, even though the heroine Maeve bonds with him. This type of conflict keeps the reader glued to the page.

Romance plot: Reverse harem books are romance books. This means they need to follow the rules of a romance. You may include elements of other genres (most commonly, reverse harem books cross over with urban fantasy, but there are also epic fantasy, science fiction, steampunk, mystery, thrillers, gothics, or more.) but at their core, these should be romance stories with a happily-ever-after. We'll talk more about plot in a later section.

Common tropes: Reverse harem isn't a genre in and of itself – it's a trope. A trope is a common theme or motif. In romance books, tropes are used to bring together the lovers and to throw up conflict. Many readers have favorite tropes, and certain tropes are eternally popular. If you want your book to succeed, it's a good idea to create your plot around other common romance tropes as well as reverse harem. We'll talk about tropes in a later section.

Whychoose: In a reverse harem book, the happily-ever-after involves the heroine settling into a relationship with *all* her guys. If she chooses a single guy – or some plot point puts all the other guys out of the picture – then it's not a reverse harem, and you'll end up with a lot of upset readers and bad reviews.

Chapter Two

HEAT LEVELS AND SEXY TIMES

Let's talk about sex! (Because of course, why else would you have purchased this book?)

Like all romance novels, reverse harem books come in all different heat levels. Imagine heat levels work on a scale of 1-5. 1 is hand-holding and maybe a chaste kiss, and 5 is lighting the bedroom on fire. At heat level 5, the characters live their emotional journey through sex, with multiple and explicitly-described sex scenes.

Let's break those heat levels down:

Level 1 (Clean/Sweet/Chaste): Think PG-rated movies. In a level 1, you might have some hand-holding, maybe a kiss, but no below-the-pants stuff and definitely no dirty thoughts or sex toys flying around.

Level 2 (Mild steam): You get some sexy feelings, intimate moments, and hot kisses, but they are brief and described mainly in terms of emotions instead of booties smooshing. Most physical intimacy happens off the page. The reader doesn't get to be inside the character's head for the whole shebang. Lots of kisses and a bit of touching, and some conversation about sex. Sex might happen, but not in front of the reader.

Level 3 (Medium steam/sexy): The middle ground. Most of us steamy writers live between here and Level 4. Expect sexy times where you get to live inside the heroine's head and feel what she feels, both emotionally and physically. The sex scenes primarily serve to further the emotional arc of the characters, and will only appear when they can do this.

Level 4 (Explicit/Scorching): This is where things can get a little kinky. In level 4 we have graphic sex and sexually-adventurous characters who want to try it all. Because of the group scenes in reverse harem, it's likely most of our books automatically get kicked up to this level. Nothing is left to the imagination, and that's the way we want it.

Level 5 (Nuclear): This is the level at which the emotional arc of the characters is linked to their sexual experience, so the whole story plays out between the sheets. Explicit language, explosive sexual tension, and probably lots of kink. Also, not a lot of external, non-sexy conflict. This is all about the world between the sheets.

Reverse harem readers use heat levels when talking about books. They also talk about 'burn'. This is the amount of time it takes the heroine and her heroes to stop dancing around each other and move their relationship to the next level. In its simplest terms, it's the amount of time between meeting and shagging, but it can also refer to sexual tension in general. There are three burn levels: slow burn, where it takes several books before any kissing or petting takes place, medium-burn, where there are sexy times in book one but maybe not full-on sex or maybe only with one member of the harem to start with, and fast burn, where things go from 0 to NC-17 in a matter of minutes!

The majority of successful reverse harem books have a heat level of between 3-5 and are medium burn. Most of them include the heroine enjoying one-on-one sexy times with each of her guys, but will also include group sex scenes where all characters are in bed together.

Both my reverse harem series have a heat level of 3-4 and are considered medium burn. There is sex in both book 1's, but it's only one-on-one and occurs later in the book. The full harem isn't established until books 2 or 3.

Two exceptions are the Veil Diaries by BL Brunnemer and the CL Stone's Ghost Bird and Scarab Beetle series. These books are young adult in tone and contain building romantic tension between characters, but no sex as yet (and in some books, no kissing). Reverse harem readers call these books slow burn or super-slow burn, and they love them just as much as the more explicit books. Our wonderful readers truly do love it all.

Make sure your heat and burn levels match the tone of your story. If your characters are in their twenties, you probably going to want a heat level of at least 3. You don't have to include group scenes, especially if you're not comfortable writing them. Some reverse harem novels only include one-on-one sex between the heroine and her harem members.

However, keep in mind that most reverse harem readers choose these books *because* they want the group sex and that group connection. Think carefully about how you're meeting reader expectations when considering how to plot your sex.

Sex scenes – even group scenes – serve a vital purpose in your book. They aren't just there to titillate the reader (that's erotica). Your sex scenes are a vital part of the romantic and emotional arc of your story. If you remove them, the story should be nonsensical.

TIPS FOR REVERSE HAREM SEX SCENES

Even if you're experienced at writing sex scenes, it can be intimidating to get hot and heavy with all these different people. If you're worried about too many cooks in the kitchen, try these tips:

- **Read widely:** Read group sex scenes written by other authors and notice how they... er... tackle the situation. You'll learn more from reading and observing than you will by setting yourself rigid rules.
- **Choose words for all the bits:** Think about your character's history and what words they might choose for all the sexy bits. Avoid purple prose, like 'love rocket' or 'flower'. Stick with the basics – cock, dick, pussy, shaft, etc. Keep it simple and let the emotions drive the scene. Beware of the word cunt as many readers don't like it.
- **Build the emotion:** The best sex scenes are all about releasing emotions. Use sex at key points in your plot as your characters become vulnerable and their physical desires get all mixed up with their wacky emotions. At the end of a sex scene, you can leave the characters (and the reader) feeling wrecked and more unsure of themselves than ever. Never leave them 100% satisfied, or they'll put the book down.
- **Think about birth control:** I believe as authors we have a responsibility to represent safe sex. You don't need to say much. The 'rustle of a condom wrapper' is enough to indicate what's going on. You can also use birth control as a plot point – for example, in Briarwood Witches, Rowan's

insistence on condoms even after all the harem has been tested is a clue about his tragic past.

- **Build tension:** A sex scene doesn't begin with one of the guys kissing the heroine or removing her blouse. It actually begins much earlier in the book. Use suggestive conversation, dirty thoughts, teasing, touching, kisses, bullying, body language, shyness, and other tools to build sexual tension through your entire story. Make the reader *beg* for that first scene.
- **Try from the male POV:** Switch things up by writing a scene from the POV of one of the heroes. Readers love being inside a man's head while he's worshipping a woman in bed.
- **What are all those guys doing?** You might need to choreograph your scene to keep all your boys busy worshipping your heroine. How can they touch/kiss/caress/penetrate her in various ways? Maybe two of them are in a relationship with each other, so they can stay busy while the others tend to their woman?
- **Keep the same style/tone:** Make sure your characters' personalities are as evident in the bedroom as they are throughout the book.
- **Your heroine should have agency:** Even though the sex in reverse harem is all about the heroine, she shouldn't just lie there and passively take her dicking. Don't fall into the trap of making the sex about the woman 'letting' them men have her body. Find ways for the woman to take charge, speak what she wants, and be involved as an active participant in her own pleasure.
- **Change it up:** Some sex is quick and dirty because your characters just can't keep their hands

> off each other. Some is slow and languid. Sometimes sex is about loving the other person, sometimes it's releasing tension. Sometimes it's losing yourself in sensation, or forgetting a horrible event, or seeking solace in a warm body. Sex can be in a bed, in the back of a car, in an empty classroom, under the stars... there are so many possibilities! Change up your sex scenes, the combinations of people, and the emotional drivers in order to keep readers interested.

Pro Tip: When I write sex scenes, I fast draft the scene first. In this draft, I include some basic actions – what's happening, who's doing what to each other, and in what order. It's like stage directions in a play. However, what I'm really focusing on is the emotional story of the characters. This initial draft includes lots of dialogue and internal thought. Once that's done, I go back over the scene a couple of times and add in description to make it extra sexy.

TO MM OR NOT MM

Even if you tightly plot your reverse harem sex scenes, you might still end up with a few guys waiting their turn. What are they going to do? Maybe they'd enjoy playing with each other...

Many reverse harem books include MM – male/male action. It's by no means essential for a reverse harem story (and some readers actively avoid books containing MM) but it adds another interesting element to the mix if you're willing to give it a try.

Personally, I think that with so many guys getting naked together and being okay with sharing one girl, it makes natural sense that at least a couple of them are also bisexual and attracted to each other.

MM works best when it arises as part of each character's emotional arc, and in a reverse harem it's vitally important that the heroine remains at the center of the relationship. All things – including male/male sexytimes – must flow from her.

In Briarwood Witches, Rowan has loved Corbin secretly ever since Corbin brought him into the coven. He sees Corbin as kind of a savior figure. But it's not until Maeve comes to the castle that her presence splits open Rowan's wounds and gives him the strength to reveal his feelings for Corbin. Maeve is able to bring the two together. The relationship is more special because they share it with Maeve, and all their key emotional moments happen while she is present and involved with both of them.

Chapter Three

PLOTTING YOUR REVERSE HAREM

In this section, we look at how to craft your reverse harem story from beginning to end.

No matter the genre of your story, the core of your reverse harem should focus on the relationship arc between the heroine and her men. In popular series that mirror the subtle deepening of feelings shown in Japanese anime (Veil Diaries, Ghost Bird), this relationship develops slowly over time from a friendship group. In other stories, sex might come first, and a relationship develops from proximity or attraction into deep love. No matter how you write your reverse harem story, it needs to follow the conventions of a romance plot.

For me, one of the biggest ways I've learned about plotting is to read the work of other authors and dissect how they build conflict, create lovable but flawed characters, and increase tension through a book. I suggest you take a look at the reading list at the back of this guide and read a few other reverse harem books to see how the experts do it.

Let's dig into plotting your reverse harem.

SERIES OR STANDALONE

Before you start plotting, it's good to know whether you're writing a single story or a series.

My advice is – write a series. While a few authors have had hits with standalone reverse harem books, the majority of reverse harem writers create a series.

It's common in romance to create a book series. However, reverse harem doesn't usually follow romance series conventions.

The typical MF romance series features one heroine and her hero in a complete arc for one book. During this book they meet, fall in love, have hot sex, discover they can't be together because of reasons (internal and/or external conflict), can't resist each other and try to be together despite reasons, experience a black moment when their happiness appears impossible, and then resolve their issues and come together for a happily ever after. Their story will be the first in the series, and the next book will introduce a new couple who experience the same arc.

These series books are linked together by the relationships of the characters. For example, book 2's hero might be the brother of book 1's hero, etc. Family members, work environments, friends, clubs, military squads, werewolf packs, and rock bands are common ways to link characters across a series. Authors hook readers into the series by teasing the future character's relationships in earlier books.

You will sometimes see this type of series in reverse harem. However, because you're creating a full romance arc for the heroine with **each one of her heroes** – as well as throwing buckets of external conflict her way, and adding a decent dose of worldbuilding (especially if it's fantasy/paranormal) – your book might end up well over 150,000 words!

For this reason, reverse harem authors commonly write

the story of one heroine and her harem across multiple books, with each book ending on a cliffhanger. These cliffhangers hook readers and leave them begging for the next book in the series. I've done this in both my series – the Briarwood Witches series completes the story of Maeve and her harem in 5 books, and the Nevermore Bookshop series is still ongoing. It will likely be 6-8 books in total, but may continue beyond that.

You should consider plotting your reverse harem story as a series in this way. Here's why:

- Readers expect series and may feel your book falls short of their other favorites if the story is too short.
- You may struggle to fit a satisfying emotional arc for each character in the harem within a single standalone book.
- If you hook readers in book one, you'll make more money on a series than with an equal number of standalone books. Readers binge-read series the way we binge-watch our favorite TV shows. If they dig your first book, they'll stick around for more.
- Series are easier to market, as you're able to make a loss offering book 1 for free or $0.99 and making up sales on sell-through of the later books.
- You can bundle your series together into a boxset, which can be a lucrative addition to your backlist.

The most common length for a reverse harem series is between 3-5 books. However, there are some as short as two books and some as long as 14+. When planning the length of your series, consider the story you want to tell, and any potential 'out' you want to give yourself if the series isn't selling.

When I planned the Briarwood Witches series, I knew from the beginning I wanted to tell Maeve's story over five books. This was in part because I wanted each book title to relate to one of the five elements of the coven's magic – earth, fire, water, air (wind), and spirit.

When I planned the Nevermore Bookshop Mysteries, I was careful to give myself an 'out', because I wasn't sure how well the series would sell. It's a cozy mystery/paranormal reverse harem mash-up and I had no idea how my readers would receive it. I decided that if the books weren't selling, I could wrap up the overarching mystery arc in four books. Luckily, they've been my bestselling series to date, so I've been able to continue the series beyond those initial four books and stretch out the mystery. I'll probably wrap up the main mystery in 6 books, but I'll keep writing about these characters as long as readers continue to enjoy them.

WORD COUNT

Because most reverse harem books are sold as ebooks with no printing cost, you have a bit of flexibility with word count. For a standard reverse harem romance novel in a series, you should be aiming at between 50,000-70,000 words per book.

Why this number? This is the standard length for a typical romance book. Your readers are used to this length. Amazon displays a page count on your book's product page where readers can see it. Some readers have a bias against books that are below 200 pages in length. 50,000 words should get you safely over 200 pages – your book will be quick to plot and write without feeling too short.

If your book is longer, it will take you more time to write, so you won't gain the benefits of releasing faster. But if you're enrolled in Kindle Unlimited, you'll earn a higher amount per book from a full read (more on this later).

Plenty of popular reverse harem books are much longer than 50-70k. The books in my Briarwood Witches series are mostly over 90,000 words. CM Stunich's *Groupie* is around 130,000 words. If readers enjoy your characters, they'll love having long books to enjoy.

Some authors have success writing short serials of 10-20k words and releasing these installments quickly (1-2 times per week). Each 'episode' of the serial ends on a cliffhanger, like a TV show. These are more popular in fantasy genres than in romance and there aren't many super successful reverse harem serials (this might simply be because there aren't yet many reverse harem serial writers). By all means, create a serial if this is your preferred type of story – but in general, full-length novels will outsell serials.

When it comes to word count, it might help you to have an idea in mind of the range you want to hit, but make the book as long as it needs to be – no longer, no shorter.

THE ROMANCE PLOT

Every romance book follows a similar plot related to the emotional journey of the characters. Different authors will break down this plot in different ways. I've written my version below, adapting it from a single MF romance to a reverse harem story.

The important thing to understand about a romance book is that characters aren't just passive onlookers who have story thrust upon them. Characters *are* your story – it's their desires, hopes, and dreams that create your plot. When creating your story, try not to worry too much about the plot itself. Instead, focus on the emotional journey of the characters.

What does this emotional journey look like? Let's take a look in the seven stages:

1. THE MEET

The meet is the initial hook/set-up of the story, where the heroine meets her lovers. The reader understands that there's an attraction, but also that the characters can't be together yet because of internal struggles and/or external conflict. This is where your tropes come into play. For example, in an enemies-to-lovers romance, the rivalry between characters prevents them from being together. This rivalry might have an external motivation (eg. destroy the new girl in CM Stunich's *Filthy Rich Boys*) but it's likely motivated by the internal emotional damage of all the characters. (We must destroy the new girl because she makes us confront ugly parts of ourselves and we can't have that).

If possible, your heroine should meet one or all of the harem members in the first chapter. This might not work with your story and is not a hard-and-fast rule. But your heroine's meeting with the harem should happen as early as possible in the book.

During the meet, you might introduce your heroine and each of her heroes separately. She'll probably meet one of them first, then the others, but not necessarily. During this stage, we begin to understand each character's longing – the thing in the book that they believe they need. This might be a dream promotion, or a magical talisman to bring their father back to life, or to overcome their grief or shyness, or to close themselves off to anyone who might care about them so they don't have to feel pain, or just to survive high school. We might see those needs clashing against each other as our heroine and heroes experience conflict.

What's important at this stage is to ensure that your heroine and all their heroes have a longing, and they also have a flaw. Their flaw prevents them from achieving what they long for, even though they may not realize it themselves yet.

In Briarwood Witches, Maeve meets Corbin in the first chapter, at the fairground where her adoptive parents are killed. She then re-meets Corbin a few chapters later, when she discovers he's one of the tenants in the castle she's inherited.

2. THE DESIRE

Here, we see what the heroine and heroes are striving for, and understand that even though they cannot see it now, they can't have what they want because of their particular flaws. We see the heroine's attraction to the heroes and their attraction to her, and understand that this attraction is somehow impossible or forbidden.

The meet and the desire are often mushed together or swapped around.

In Briarwood Witches, we learn about Maeve's desire right from the beginning – to go to college, study physics, and become an astronaut. However, she can't achieve this goal until she reconciles her logical mind with her supernatural powers and learns to stop seeing the world in black/white, right/wrong.

3. FIRST TURNING POINT

This is where the characters start to strive for their goal. In a reverse harem romance, the plot will primarily focus on the heroine's goal, or on a collective goal for the harem. However, each character will have their own goals.

The characters cannot achieve their goal, however, because their flaw holds them back. This might manifest as either an external 'baddie' (the antagonist) thwarting their plans or internally as conflict that holds them back.

At this stage, it's impossible for your characters to achieve their goal.

In Briarwood Witches, you see this as Maeve wanting to sell the castle and go to university. She can't do this because of her inability to embrace her powers. She can't believe in magic, and so the magical world (the external plot of the fae) won't allow her to leave.

4. RAISING THE STAKES

This is where shit gets real. The heroine and heroes deepen their relationship. They move closer toward their goal. They see what life could be like after they've achieved it. There's a real shot at happiness and acceptance and all that good stuff.

However, you (the author) still know how impossible this is, because the characters are living a lie. They haven't overcome their flaws. They're hiding things from each other. They're still vulnerable and scared. And the external problems or the real world are closing in. Their flaws are still pushing them back.

In Briarwood Witches, this is the entirely of books 1-3. Again and again, Maeve and her harem strive to return Briarwood to normal, but everything they do just makes their situation more dire.

5. THE POINT OF NO RETURN

This is another turning point, but it's different from the others because it's at this point that the characters have learned so much about themselves that they can't go back to the way things were before, even if they tried. In some books, they do try, but it's impossible because they're no longer the same people.

Your heroine and her heroes have not yet overcome their

flaws, but they're starting to. In Briarwood, the point of no return is actually when Maeve meets her mother, and how that happening changes the relationship she has with her harem. It changes what she thought she knew about family. The actual return of Maeve's mother from the dead is also a *literal* point of no return – now that she's been brought back Maeve can no longer deny the role of magic in her life.

6. DARK MOMENT

This is when the heroine and the reader believe that all is lost. Maybe the harem has broken up, or they believe there is no way to win. This has to be a true crisis without an obvious or easy solution, or the reader will feel cheated.

Everything explodes as the characters come face-to-face with their flaws in the ugliest and most harrowing way.

In a reverse harem, the heroine may have the dark moment with members of the harem individually throughout the series, but they will come together at the end to face some external struggle. In Briarwood Witches, each of the men has their own dark moment throughout the series, and the final dark moment belongs to Maeve. She needs the strength of all five of her men in order to find the strength to do what she has to do.

In Briarwood Witches, the main dark moment is Corbin's death. The coven believes they are strong, but when they lose Corbin they discover that all their strength came from him, and not from themselves. They fall to pieces and it seems impossible for there to be any happiness without Corbin

7. HAPPILY EVER AFTER

The heroine uses her own skills and the support of her harem in order to save the day. Or the harem realizes how much they need the heroine and fly in at the last moment to save her. There's an emotionally-satisfying conclusion and everyone lives happily ever after.

The happily ever after can only happen when the heroine and every member of their harem overcome their initial flaws to be together. Often, it is the strength of the bond of the harem and their love for the heroine that heal the men.

Maeve and her harem each uncover their own hidden strength. They travel to the underworld, save Corbin, and find a unique solution to the problem of the fae. Each member of the harem has their own happily-ever-after, not only in love, but also by uncovering and celebrating their strengths in new ways.

Pro tip: remember that with several heroes in the book, your heroine might reach a turning point with different characters at different times. This helps to keep the tension mounting during the series – just when one relationship seems rock-solid, another character has a crisis. Conflict is what makes a series interesting, and in reverse harem you can pack a mountain of conflict into a tiny book!

REVERSE HAREM PLOT/CHARACTER CONFLICT

If your characters met, had sex, fell in love, then lived happily ever after, your readers would be bored. A story needs conflict in order to get the reader to invest in the characters and grow attached to their struggles.

Think about what's going to cause conflict in your story. Here are some common plot and character themes from reverse harem books that can be sources of conflict. This is not an exhaustive list, but it might stimulate some of your own ideas. You might like to include:

- One of the guys resists the idea of being part of

the harem. He doesn't want to share the heroine, and part of his character arc is to release this possessive urge. I use this for Arthur in the Briarwood Witches series.

- The heroine is the 'chosen one' for some kind of magical society, with special powers she doesn't know she possessed. She has to learn how to use these powers, and her guys are her guardians or teachers. She may reject her powers and try to live a normal life.
- The heroine needs magic/power/love from an outside source in order to reach her full potential. Usually, that source is one other person, but for some reason there's an accident/fault, and now it's several people. She may deal with societal pressure and ostracism because of this.
- The heroine is royalty/important/upper class and in need of protection from a band of soldiers/guardians. These types of novels use the forced proximity trope and often deal with forbidden romance between different classes.
- The heroine is captured by a group of secret agents/cops/criminals, who she comes to care for. These are often dark romances featuring dubious-consent and Stockholm syndrome.
- Revenge – the heroine may be seeking revenge for a wrong done to her, and hires or uses the guys to help her do it, or she may be taking revenge on the guys and accidentally falls for them instead. CM Stunich's *Filthy Rich Boys* or Cora Lee June's *Lies and Other Drugs* use revenge as a key theme.
- Fated mates – the heroine experiences a magical connection to the men in her harem, and must come to terms with their world, which will be new

to her. Fated mates are common in shifter stories, and often deals with animal instinct vs higher thought.

- Arranged marriages – a cultural or religious tradition/family obligation ties the heroine to a group of men. Usually, these are also enemies-to-lovers stories where the heroine starts off hating the heroes and then grows to love them through shared adversity.
- Fairytale retellings – traditional fairy tales, legends, and myths are twisted and retold with a reverse harem bent. These stories are rife with family conflict and magical worlds colliding. Check out Marie Robinson's *House of Secrets* for a great example.
- The heroine struggles to fit in at her academy, workplace, court, etc, which provides a ton of conflict. The guys become her friends and confidants and help her to navigate this world she's found herself in.
- The heroine was friends with the boys when they were all children. For some reason, they are all separated and find each other again as adults. Sparks fly, but the reason they were separated will haunt them. See Eva Chase's *Witch's Consorts* series.

Pro tip: Usually, the heroes in a reverse harem novel already know each other. They may be friends, bandmates, soldiers in the same unit, or part of a tribe or pack. This makes it much easier for you to set up the story and move onto the meatier parts of the book.

In other books, the heroine acquires the guys one-by-one, or a combination thereof. In my Briarwood Witches series, Maeve meets four of her five men when she first arrives at

Briarwood Castle, and they've already forged a deep friendship. The fifth guy, Blake, is a witch raised by the fae who follows Maeve back from the fae realm. His trickster ways and the fact that he was raised fae means the other guys distrust him. Even though Maeve accepts him into the coven, it takes the others time to befriend him.

COMMON TROPES

We've already spoken a little about tropes in reverse harem. Tropes are themes and devices used in a plot. In romance, tropes are usually used to bring the characters together or create a conflict in their impending relationship. There are lots of common tropes that readers love and actively look for.

Reverse harem is a trope. However, you can combine it with other common romance tropes for maximum conflict and readability. Readers unfamiliar with reverse harem will be more likely to pick up your book if it deals with another common romance trope, and you improve your chances of success.

What are some common romance tropes you can use in your reverse harem story?

FORCED PROXIMITY

Characters who can't stand each other or are completely different are thrown together with no way out except to cooperate.

You need a reason why all these characters are thrown together and why the guys choose to focus on this one girl. Often, there's a paranormal/magical reason for the connection – in KT Strange's Rogue Witch series, Darcy is a witch working as a band manager who is forced to manage the werewolf band Phoenixcry. Throwing these two feuding magical races together on a tiny tour bus is the heart of the story's initial conflict.

ENEMIES-TO-LOVERS

This trope often goes hand-in-hand with forced proximity. The sparring leads of the novel realize they have the hots for each other. Hatred and passion combine on the page and the result is explosive. Enemies-to-lovers is perhaps the most common romance trope.

CHILDHOOD FRIENDS/HOMECOMING

In this series, the heroine and her guys were friends as children. For some reason, they are separated (perhaps the heroine moves away, or their parents forbid them to talk to each other, etc). They meet again as adults and their childhood friendship blossoms into romance. However, whatever tore them apart the first time still threatens their love. Eva Chase has a series called Witch's Consorts which uses this childhood friends theme.

FORBIDDEN LOVE

This is your classic Romeo and Juliet tale. The children of warring families fall in love, or your heroine and heroes are of different classes or races. Whatever the reason, their relationship will bring a world of trouble down on their own heads, but they cannot stay away from each other. KT Strange's Rogue Witch series uses forbidden love as a source of conflict.

FAKE RELATIONSHIP/MARRIAGE OF CONVENIENCE

This is a super popular trope in historical romance books, but hasn't been used to great effect in reverse harem (probably because it's currently illegal in western cultures to marry more than one person). That's good news – it means you have lots of scope, especially if you write a paranormal world where the normal rules don't apply.

In this trope, the heroine and hero/es agree to pretend to be in a relationship for mutual benefits (usually monetary or to get other family members off their back). However, during the course of this fake marriage, they uncover real feelings for each other.

ACADEMY

This is more of a fantasy trope than a romance trope, but it's popular in reverse harem so I've included it in the guide. In an academy book, your heroine finds herself in an elite (and possibly magical) school. She has to navigate the politics of this new academic system and its students (who inevitably hate her), with the heroes as her allies/adversaries. For a great example, try *Wishing for them* by Ellabee Andrews or the Phoenix Academy series by Lucy Auburn.

Other common tropes in romance are blackmail, best friend's sibling, arranged marriages, class warfare, guardian/ward, kidnappings, mail-order brides, falling through a portal, revenge, or the secret/lost heir to a throne or mighty fortune. Common character types for heroes are athletes, billionaires, cowboys, soldiers/guardians, royalty, vampires, werewolves (and other shapeshifters) fae, and other supernatural creatures.

Pro tip: Most reverse harem novels have some kind of paranormal element. It's easier to set up a harem if there's a magic-based reason for it to exist. If you're writing contemporary novels set in the real world, it can be more difficult to figure out scenarios where a harem might develop (and how the members can have their happily-ever-after).

Look for groups of men who might normally co-exist together, especially if they exist outside the norms of society – roommates, band members, sports teams, colleagues, Navy SEALs, motorcycle gangs, doomsday preppers, etc.

Chapter Four

MARKETING YOUR REVERSE HAREM BOOK

One of the reasons I think my reverse harem books have done well is because I'm a fan of the genre first, and a writer second. I didn't start writing these books to make a quick buck – I poured my heart and soul into creating a story that was incredibly personal to me and that would make readers happy.

When it came to marketing my series, a lot of what I've done was second-nature because I already had a small audience from my previous books and I was already talking about reverse harem books as a reader in the largest Facebook groups. The core reader group for this genre is still small, so if you involve yourself in the community early on, you stand the best chance of engaging them with your book when it comes out.

In this section, I've included some tips on marketing your reverse harem series, including your title, cover, blurb, and launch strategy. It's definitely not an exhaustive list, but I hope it will give you some idea of what has/hasn't worked for me.

PRE-LAUNCH

What do you need to do before you launch your book in order to give it the best possible chance of success? Let's find out:

CHOOSE YOUR PEN NAME

The first step is to decide on the name to author your reverse harem. You might like to use your own name. However, if you have conservative relatives or are concerned about what work colleagues might say when they discover your books, you might consider using a pen name.

Each pen name you have (and many authors have many) should encompass books that appeal to the same broad audience. That way, your readers won't be surprised by sudden changes in genre. If it's romance and the heat level is similar, you can include it under one name.

Do you need a specific pen name just for your reverse harem books? My answer is, it depends. I personally don't consider reverse harem to be its own genre. I think reverse harem is a trope in romance. For this reason, I launched my own reverse harem books under my established paranormal romance pen name.

However, if your current pen name publishes outside the romance/urban fantasy genres, I'd consider starting a fresh name. You don't want your young adult thriller readers getting confused!

REVERSE HAREM COVERS

As most reverse harem readers will first notice your book by seeing the cover in thumbnail, you need to create a bold design that stands out. Begin by compiling a list of reverse harem books and their covers. Look for elements that are similar between them. What colors do they use? What motifs are present? How many figures are in the scene? What other objects are present? How is the genre portrayed? What types of font are used for the title and author name?

As well as studying reverse harem covers, think about the additional genres and tropes you've included in your works. Look at covers of authors who write similar books and include the common details to signal to readers the type of story they could expect.

For paranormal reverse harem books, the general trend is for a woman as the central figure. Depending on how the book is written, this figure might be in a power pose with some badass outfit and a weapon, ala urban fantasy. Or it might be a girl in a beautiful dress. The magical aspects of the genre might be shown by magical flares and flashes, by animals (to represent shifters), or other clues/props.

For contemporary, the covers are often similar to other contemporary novels. They might include a central figure and some elements to allude to the other tropes – athletic equipment for a sports romance, gates for an academy book, etc. Some novels, like CM Stunich's *Filthy Rich Boys*, include only typographic and design elements without a figure.

Some covers will also include bare-chested men (manchest). Although manchest covers usually sell bad boy romance novels, they're more difficult to do in reverse harem stories because it's hard to create an attractive composition with so many figures.

Hard, but not impossible. Talk to your cover designer about options and let them work their magic. Remember, it's vital to your success to have a great cover.

BLURB

As well as hooking them with the other tropes you've used, your blurb needs to alert the reader to the fact your book is reverse harem. The key reason readers turn to reverse harem is because they don't want to read a love triangle where the heroine has to choose. Make this very clear.

The key to a good reverse harem blurb – and it's the same for any blurb – is to go light on the plot details and heavy on the relationship/character conflict. What's the relationship tension? How does the harem factor into the plot? What's the internal conflict the heroine is struggling with and how does this create conflict with the harem?

Here's an example from my blurb for *A Dead and Stormy Night*:

> ***What do you get when you cross a cursed bookshop, three hot fictional men, and a punk rock heroine nursing a broken heart?***
>
> *After being fired from her fashion internship in New York City, Mina Wilde decides it's time to reevaluate her life. She returns to the quaint English village where she grew up to take a job at the local bookshop, hoping that being surrounded by great literature will help her heal from a devastating blow.*
>
> *But Mina soon discovers her life is stranger than fiction – a mysterious curse on the bookshop brings fictional characters to life in lust-worthy bodies. Mina finds herself babysitting Poe's raven, making hot dogs for Heathcliff, and getting IT help from James Moriarty, all while trying not to fall for the three broken men who should only exist within her imagination.*

> *When Mina's ex-best friend shows up dead with a knife in her back, she's the chief suspect. She'll have to solve the murder if she wants to clear her name. Will her fictional boyfriends be able to keep her out of prison?*
>
> *The Nevermore Bookshop Mysteries are what you get when all your book boyfriends come to life. Join a brooding antihero, a master criminal, a cheeky raven, and a heroine with a big heart (and an even bigger book collection) in this brand new steamy reverse harem paranormal romance mystery series by* USA Today *bestselling author Steffanie Holmes.*

I'm not going to pretend to be a blurb expert, but I think this one is not too bad. This is my most popular book/series ever, and I think in part it's because of this blurb. Why does it work?

a) It's clear from the first line that it's a reverse harem story.

b) The first line is a strong, bold hook – I like to use lists to create hooks in this way.

c) I give some brief details about the plot. Mina moves home, works at a bookshop, and has to solve a murder. However, that stuff all happens in the first few chapters. I don't waste time in the blurb talking about anything too deep into the book, or telling you Mina's best friend's name. Plot details are sparse because all they're really doing is alerting the reader to expect a murder mystery.

d) What really pulls the reader in is the hints about Mina's internal emotions – about the 'devastating blow' and about her relationship with all three of the guys. This makes it obvious that this is more than just a mystery book.

e) I use common keywords readers understand, such as reverse harem, paranormal romance, etc.

f) I have heaps of fun hooks. "When all your book

boyfriends come to life" is a line I use in my FB/AMS ads to draw reader attention to the book.

It's a good idea to test different blurbs. Testing blurbs is never going to be a perfect science because Amazon won't give you traffic data. Using two different blurbs for a FB ad can help you see which blurb performs better in terms of click-through. For *The Castle of Earth and Embers*, I've tested two different versions – one in third person, and one in first. Here they are:

Blurb 1:

> ***Maeve Crawford has her life mathematically calculated down to the last detail; Leave her podunk Arizona town, graduate MIT, get into the space program, be the first woman on Mars, read lots of books, get a cat (not necessarily in this order).***
>
> *All Maeve's careful plans come crashing down when her parents are killed in a freak accident, and she discovers she's inherited a real, honest-to-goodness English castle – complete with turrets, ramparts, and four gorgeous male tenants.*
>
> *Corbin – the protector wallowing in guilt*
>
> *Arthur – the warrior tired of fighting*
>
> *Flynn – the trickster with an artist's soul*
>
> *Rowan – the enigma whose scars run deep*
>
> *As soon as Maeve enters Briarwood, she's drawn to Corbin, Arthur, Flynn, and Rowan – four beautiful boys drenched in grief, hope, and ancient magic. Maeve needs them all to heal her broken heart, and*

they need her to help them protect the world from the fae host baying at the castle gates.

Dark forces converge on Briarwood castle, and Maeve Crawford – science geek, scarred soul, lover of four remarkable men – must draw from herself a power she never imagined in order to protect the shattered remains of her life.

The Castle of Earth and Embers is the first in a brand new steamy reverse harem romance by USA Today *bestselling author, Steffanie Holmes. This full-length book glitters with love, heartache, hope, grief, dark magic, fairy trickery, steamy scenes, British slang, meat pies, second chances, and the healing powers of a good cup of tea. Read on only if you believe one just isn't enough.*

Blurb 2:

Dear Fae,

Don't even THINK about attacking my castle.

This science geek witch and her four magic-wielding men are about to get medieval on your ass.

I'm Maeve Crawford. For years I've had my future mathematically calculated down to the last detail; Leave my podunk Arizona town, graduate MIT, get into the space program, be the first woman on Mars, get a cat (not necessarily in this order).

Then fairies killed my parents and shot the whole plan to hell.

I've inherited a real, honest-to-goodness English castle – complete with turrets, ramparts, and four gorgeous male tenants, who I'm totally not in love with.

Not at all.

It would be crazy to fall for four guys at once, even though they're totally gorgeous and amazing and wonderful and kind.

But not as crazy as finding out I'm a witch. A week ago, I didn't even believe magic existed, and now I'm up to my ears in spells and prophetic dreams and messages from the dead.

When we're together – and I'm talking in the Biblical sense – the five of us wield a powerful magic that can banish the fae forever. They intend to stop us by killing us all.

I can't science my way out of this mess.

Forget NASA, it's going to take all my smarts just to survive Briarwood Castle.

The Castle of Earth and Embers is the first in a brand new steamy reverse harem romance by USA Today *bestselling author, Steffanie Holmes. This full-length book glitters with love, heartache, hope, grief, dark magic, fairy trickery, steamy scenes, British slang, meat pies, second chances, and the healing powers of a good cup of tea. Read on only if you believe one just isn't enough.*

You can see how both blurbs give the same general information, but with a different tone. You may be surprised – or not – to learn that blurb 2 tested better in the Facebook ads, so that's the blurb I now use.

Read blurbs from other popular reverse harem books and look for patterns. You'll notice hooky first tines, lots of short, snappy sentences, liberal lashings of sexual tension, and a lot of laundry lists (in the same vein as my closing paragraphs). Pay particular attention to the way different authors bring the reverse harem aspect to life and use only a few words to portray a complex relationship.

Don't copy directly (that's shitty and also a copyright violation), but you can use the structure and descriptions in other blurbs as a jumping-off point for your own work.

HITTING THE TROPES

A big part of marketing your reverse harem book is making sure you've hit the tropes that readers are looking for. All the marketing in the world will not make a book rise to the top if it's not something readers want to read. Before you launch, look at your book as a marketer instead of an author, and ask yourself if you need to edit it to make it more appealing to readers. You might also get a friend you trust to read it over and point out how you can improve.

This may seem weird, but for many of my books, I will write the blurb before I write the actual book. That helps me to see if I'm really writing a hooky story or if I'm kidding myself.

KINDLE UNLIMITED OR WIDE?

Your next big pre-launch consideration is whether you want to enrol your reverse harem book into Kindle Unlimited, or have it available on all stores.

Kindle Unlimited is Amazon's "Spotify for books" program. Readers pay a set monthly fee ($10 in the US) to download and read as many books as they want from the KU catalog. Authors who enrol their books in KU are paid a certain amount per page each time a reader turns the page in KU (And the pages are standardized over all books to make it fair). The page rate varies per month but is usually between $0.0040-$0.0048 per page.

Depending on the length of your book and the price you set, you'll usually earn a little less for a full KU-read than you would if the reader purchased the ebook outright.

In order to enrol in Kindle Unlimited, you have to be exclusive to Amazon. Each KU 'term' is for 90 days, so you enrol for three months and then you can pull your book out and take it wide if you want.

Being Amazon-exclusive means you can't have your ebook on sale on iBooks, Kobo, or any other stores. The disadvantage to Kindle Unlimited is that you put all your eggs into one basket. The advantage is that you have access to the vast number of voracious readers who devour reverse harem books in Kindle Unlimited.

For a new author, Kindle Unlimited is a great option, as it gives readers an avenue to 'sample' your writing without having to plonk down their hard-earned cash (as they've already paid for their subscription). The readers feel as though your book is 'free' and so they're more likely to take a chance on a new-to-them author than if they had to pay $2.99+ for your book.

It's up to you whether you enrol your book in Kindle Unlimited or put it on sale across all platforms. For reverse harem, I strongly recommend you consider Kindle Unlimited for at least the first three months. The vast majority of readers in the genre use this service, and it will help you build an audience. You can always take your books wide later if you find Kindle Unlimited isn't working for you.

YOUR BOOK LAUNCH

The most important time for marketing your new reverse harem book is during its launch month. This is when the most eyeballs will be on your book and when Amazon will be promoting it to their audience. Here are some tips to help you rock your reverse harem launch:

FACEBOOK

Right now, reverse harem as a genre has an active presence on Facebook. This is changing, as more people are writing books and the large reader groups are starting to get flooded with authors promoting their books. As this becomes more prevalent, readers will start to avoid the groups.

But that hasn't happened yet. For now, reverse harem Facebook groups are a great place to introduce yourself to the community, and to network with other authors. I suggest you join some of the biggest groups and apply for a slot for a Takeover (this is where you have exclusive posting rights in the group for an hour to introduce readers to your new book). These will help alert readers to your work.

Also, if you have your own Facebook reader group or page, don't forget to alert them about your release! Your fans want to know when you've written something new, even if not all of them will follow you into reverse harem.

You can use Facebook to run ads targeting new readers. Facebook ads are a steep learning curve and I would recommend holding off on using them until you have a deeper understanding of the genre and your goals as an author.

MAILING LIST

If you don't already have a mailing list, now is a good time to set one up. Most writers use services like Mailerlite or Mailchimp, however there are literally hundreds to choose from.

Once your list is set up, link it in the back of your book, and readers will sign up to be alerted when you have a new release. I like to offer readers an exclusive scene or free story in exchange for their email address. This helps encourage more people to sign up. I can then use these lists to create targeted lookalike audiences for my Facebook ads.

For my previous non-RH romance releases, I've used a free bonus epilogue giving the readers a happily-ever-after scene (usually with some serious teasers for the next book). For the Briarwood Witches series, I wrote a full 12k word short story featuring Maeve and one of her men set a couple of years before the start of book 1. When I tested the numbers against those from my last books, I found that there wasn't a significant increase in the number of people signing up to the newsletter for a full story versus the scene. I decided that was a lot of work for no real gain, so I won't do a full story again.

For the Nevermore Bookshop Mysteries, I wrote out a key scene from book one from the point-of-view for a different character. The scene was originally in Mina's POV. I changed it up to be in the POV of one of her guys, Quoth. It hints at a few mysteries Mina isn't aware of. It was simple and quick to write (because the scene was written for Mina already) and has been extremely effective!

If you already have readers on your mailing list, then you should alert them about your new release. I do two alerts – one on release day, one a few days later because people often don't see emails.

You can also ask other authors to promote your book to their lists. We call this a 'newsletter swap'. It's most effective if the audience for your book and the other author's books is as close as possible. I have a few long-term author friends who I swap with on a regular basis and it always adds a boost.

Pro tip: Keep a separate list or group within your main list of readers who enjoy reverse harem. I collect my readers from the back of my reverse harem books. I send out newsletters to this list first, before my larger list. Doing this helps Amazon to learn that my books are similar to other reverse harem books, and means I'm more likely to be advertised alongside other reverse harem titles in also-broughts and in searches.

AMS ADS

AMS ads are pay-per-click ads operated by Amazon. They allow you to bid against other authors for better placement in search results, in the 'sponsored products' section located on each book product page, and on the lockscreens of Kindles.

AMS ads can take a lot of fiddling to figure out. Your first step is to compile keyword lists of book titles, authors, and keyword searches related to your books. Look for similar reverse harem authors and reverse harem keywords. Once you have this list, write some short and snappy ad copy (I usually choose the hooky sentences in my blurbs as the starting point) and test different ads with a small budget ($3-5 per day) and a low bid ($0.15-0.20). Over time you will start to notice what works and what doesn't.

Be aware that Amazon does not allow the words 'reverse harem', 'harem', and any description that implies your book contains a polyamorous relationship in your AMS ad copy. This includes the title, series title, and subtitle of your book and on your cover.

You'll need to consider if it's worthwhile for you to include 'reverse harem' on your cover or in your series name. My Briarwood Witches series was originally called 'Briarwood Reverse Harem' but I changed it so I could run AMS ads (which I haven't found very effective, so I'm not certain the change was worthwhile).

GIVEAWAYS

I've been having a lot of success running themed giveaways based on details from my books. For example, I ran this mega giveaway to celebrate the final book release in the Briarwood Witches series. I included a gift from every character in the harem that suited their personality.

Picture: Social media image of the items in my Briarwood Witches mega swag giveaway.

I use the site King Sumo (kingsumo.com) to set up the giveaway. I usually run them for 3-4 weeks. On King Sumo, participants can get additional entries for completing different tasks. I offer additional entries for people who visit the book's page on Amazon, sign up for my mailing list, join my author group, and follow me on Instagram. Each time I run one, I add a few hundred new people on each of those platforms.

I send these giveaways out to my mailing list and promote them on my Facebook page/group and on my blog. I also ask other authors if I can add the giveaway on their Facebook groups. Then I can announce the release of my new book on those platforms and capture readers' attention.

Chapter Five

BUILDING YOUR AUDIENCE

If you want to keep releasing reverse harem books, then it helps to have an audience of eager readers ready to snap them up.

Your reverse harem audience will build over time as you release more books and word gets around the community about how awesome you are.

However, there are things you can do to help build and maintain that audience of fans, so that they're excited about your next release and actively spreading the word about your awesomeness. I've found this the most effective marketing strategy for growing my profile in reverse harem – especially important when you don't have a huge advertising budget to throw around.

NEWSLETTER

As discussed in the previous section, your newsletter is a valuable tool for capturing fans and alerting them about new releases. However, you can also use it as a tool for connecting with your fans by mailing out fun teasers, competitions and giveaways, behind-the-scenes author stuff, and fun games and trivia.

Use the tools provided by your mailing list service to test how often you can send your newsletter and which types of content are most popular. Compare open rates and click-through rates and create a schedule that works for you.

Your newsletter is one of your most valuable assets. **You own it.** A social media site could change their algorithms or disappear completely overnight – destroying everything you've built. However, your newsletter list is yours forever. For this reason, it should be your first choice for audience building.

READER GROUP

As well as a newsletter, it's good to have someplace online for readers to congregate for updates and fun. In reverse harem, reader groups are usually on Facebook, and the authors post a couple of times a day about book progress, tease covers and excerpts, talk about random facts related to the book, ask questions, run polls, do giveaways, and play silly games.

If you want to see a reader group in action, feel free to join mine – Books that Bite on Facebook.

What kinds of things can you post in your reader group?

- Teasers from your upcoming release.
- Cover reveals.
- Announcements (new releases, pre-orders, paperbacks available, appearances, etc).
- Predictive text games (getting readers to finish a sentence with predictive text).
- Choosing games (giving readers 5 pictures and getting them to choose one).
- Playlists and songs that relate to your books.

- Fun facts about your books.
- Behind-the-scenes in your writer cave.
- Pictures of your pets (these are always popular).
- Word count goals.
- Promo for other authors books you think your readers will like.
- Surveys/polls about your books.
- Spoiler/discussion threads (where readers can talk about a recently released book).
- Like video streams of you on release day (eating cake, drinking absinthe, or otherwise celebrating!)

BOX SETS AND COLLECTIONS

As you publish more books in your series, you're able to bundle them together into collections and boxsets. You can sell these boxsets as additional products on Amazon and the other platforms, and they're a great tool for attracting readers and re-igniting interest in a flagging series.

The best time to release a boxset is when sales/page reads on the single titles begin to flag. Because you offer the boxset at a discount (my 5-book Briarwood Witches box set is $9.99, whereas the individual books are $4.99 each), the box set sales will cannibalize interest in the other books.

You can offer a box set of the entire series or – if it's a longer series – just the first three books. If you have a lot of different series, you might like to create a 'starter library' box set of the first books in all your different series.

MULTI-AUTHOR BOX SETS

Multi-author box sets are when a group of authors gets together to create a box set. These sets usually sell for $0.99 and offer readers 10-20 novels – one each from the participating authors. Each author will then get the chance to promo the next book in their series or another release at the end of their novel.

Multi-author box sets are a great deal for readers because they get so many books for such a low price, and they might discover new authors to follow. For authors, they offer you the chance to get your name in front of a large number of new readers.

As Amazon tightens the rules around these sets, multi-author box sets have waned in popularity. However, since 2017 there have been several reverse harem sets that have done exceptionally well. You may like to consider a box set as an option to expand your readership or promote a popular series.

Most box sets will be in Kindle Unlimited, and they will require you to submit a novel that is not only exclusive to Amazon, but exclusive to the box set (for a limited time). Some authors will unpublish their first-in-series book for a limited time in order to place that in the box set. However, this may confuse readers who stumble on your series but can't find book one.

More commonly, authors will submit the first book in a new series. They might use the box set as a way to 'test' the market for a new series idea. They may write a short novella and then expand that idea into a novel later if there's enough reader interest.

Alternatively, an author might write a spin-off novella or novel featuring characters in an already established series.

If you're submitting a book to a box set, look for sets that are exclusively for reverse harem novels. This ensures you're targeting the most relevant audience. Look for sets that focus on reaching as many readers as possible as their primary goal. You want to introduce yourself to new readers, who may go on to read the rest of your series.

Participating in a multi-author box set is a lot of work. You'll be expected to perform duties like advertising the set and participating in group promos. You may also pay a fee in order to be part of the set (this fee will cover paid promotion of the set). Make sure you have the time and money to commit before jumping in, and that your set owner operates a professional set with contracts and acceptable terms. Authors have been caught out by box-set scammers and unprofessional presentation before, so ask around about the reputation of the set organizer, trust your instincts, and keep everything in writing.

IN-PERSON READER EVENTS

Many reverse harem writers enjoy meeting their readers in real life at signing events and conventions.

When considering in-person events, carefully weigh up cost/benefit to make sure you're going to get value for money. Some events ask you to sponsor reader swag or give away a certain amount of books. Others require you to stay at a specific hotel that might add significantly to your costs. As a self-published author, you'll also be paying to print and ship boxes of your books for signing. It's important that all this investment is recouped. Don't just sign up for events to appease your own vanity about being an invited author – put that money toward top-notch covers and editing for your next release.

Always ask yourself, will this event deepen my relationship with my readers? What am I gaining by participating? How many readers will actually show up?

Chapter Six

WHAT NEXT?

Now that you've released your reverse harem book and you're growing your audience, what should you do next?

WRITE THE NEXT BOOK

The sooner you get the second book in your reverse harem series (you are writing a series, aren't you?) the more likely you are to capture those hungry readers before they forget about the story.

Many reverse harem writers (myself included) are publishing books at the rate of one every 6-8 weeks. Some are even faster. You should go at your own pace and write a story that's compelling, but you may like to investigate ways to increase your daily word count to improve your speed.

As a full-time author, increasing my daily word count has been one of the most valuable skills I've learned.

Pro tip: Rachel Aaron has a great book called *2k to 10k: Writing Faster, Writing Better, and Writing More of What You Love* about increasing your word count that might be useful.

INTERACT WITH READERS

Between book releases, keep reader interest alive by posting regularly in your author group, sending out newsletters, and interacting in the main reverse harem groups on Facebook. Make sure no one has time to forget your name!

GROW YOUR GROUP/NEWSLETTER

Use giveaways, author takeovers, and paid promotions to grow your email list, reader group, and social media. If you can increase these numbers between launches, you can improve sales of your series as you add more books.

TRY A SALE

Once you have more than three books in your reverse harem series, you might like to experiment with putting book one on sale for a few days. If your book is enrolled in Kindle Unlimited, you can schedule up to 5 free days during every 3-month period, or a countdown deal where you can price your book at $0.99 and keep 70% royalties (as opposed to the 35% you'd normally expect at that price point).

If your book is wide, you can set your books to free on the other platforms and wait for Amazon to price-match it, and you can set a sales amount for $0.99.

You may like to use newsletter services like FreeBooksy, Bookbub, Robin Reads, and Red Feather Romance to promote your sale.

HAVE FUN!

Don't lose sight of why you're writing and publishing reverse harem – because it's fun and because you have unique stories to tell.

I've never been happier than when I've been exploring the worlds I've created and the remarkable characters who inhabit them. I love the challenge of making everyone smoosh booties and overcome obstacles to achieve their happily ever after.

Reverse harem is regular romance on steroids. We get to explore a fascinating relationship dynamic and write about strong, sassy women who command the devotion of amazing men. We get to be fantasy-spinners and dream-makers, and it's damn cool.

So what are you waiting for? Get started on your reverse harem romance novel today.

REVERSE HAREM READING LIST

I've compiled this list of some of my favorite reverse harem books, many of which I've mentioned in this guide.

In order to effectively write in any genre, you need to understand its conventions and tropes, so you know what readers want. If you haven't already devoured several reverse harem books, I suggest you choose a few titles off this list and get started:

Steffanie Holmes, Briarwood Witches series (paranormal witches/fae)

Book 1, *The Castle of Earth and Embers.*

Steffanie Holmes, Nevermore Bookshop Mysteries series (paranormal literary heroes)

Book 1, *A Dead and Stormy Night.*

Bethany Jadin, The Code series (action, romantic suspense)

Book 1, *Vested Interest.*

. . .

Marie Robinson, Beautiful Secrets series (paranormal, fairy-tale retelling)

Book 1, *House of Secrets.*

Katya Moore, Arysia Bellmont series (paranormal, dragon shifters)

Book 1, *Shadow on the Wing.*

CM Stunich, Rock Hard Beautiful series (contemporary rockstar)

Book 1, *Groupie.*

KT Strange, Rogue Witch series (paranormal rockstar)

Book 1, *Phoenixcry.*

B L Brunnemer, Veil Diaries (paranormal young adult)

Book 1, *Trying to Live With The Dead.*

CL Stone, Scarab Beetle series (young adult)

Book 1, *Thief.*

Tate James, Kit Davenport series (paranormal)

Book 1, *Vixen's Lead.*

Jaymin Eve, Curse of the Gods series (paranormal gods)

Book 1, *Trickery.*

. . .

Kristy Cunning, All The Pretty Monsters series (paranormal vampire)

Book 1, *Gypsy Blood.*

Eva Chase, Witch's Consorts series (paranormal gothic)

Book 1, *Consort of Secrets.*

Joely Sue Burkhart, Their Vampire Queen series (paranormal vampire)

Book 1, *Queen Takes Knights.*

Alex Liddell, Power of Five series (paranormal fae)

Book 1, *Power of Five.*

ABOUT THE AUTHOR

Steffanie Holmes writes steamy paranormal romance with a touch of the gothic. She's the award-winning and bestselling author of more than 30 books, including the popular reverse harem series – The Briarwood Witches and the Nevermore Bookshop Mysteries.

In 2017, Steff was awarded the Attitude Award for Artistic Achievement, in recognition of her work as a writer with a disability. In 2018 she was a finalist for a New Zealand woman of influence.

Before becoming a writer, Steffanie worked as an archaeologist and museum curator. She loves to explore myth, magic, and ancient conceptions of love. From Dark Age Europe to crumbling gothic estates, Steffanie is fascinated with how love can blossom between the most unlikely characters.

Steffanie lives in New Zealand with her husband and a horde of cantankerous cats.

Come hang with Steffanie
www.steffanieholmes.com
hello@steffanieholmes.com

www.ingramcontent.com/pod-product-compliance
Ingram Content Group UK Ltd.
Pitfield, Milton Keynes, MK11 3LW, UK
UKHW040012200726
13854UKWH00001B/170

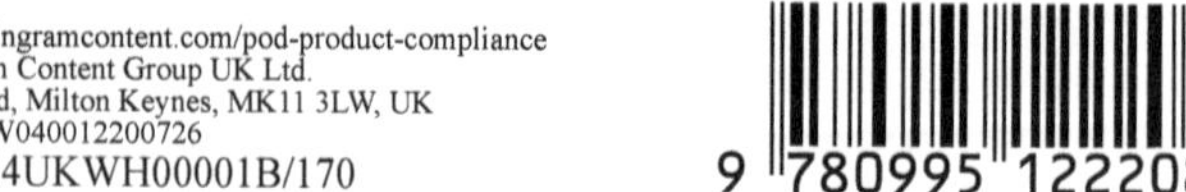